THE
Hindu-American
MOSAIC

The American Hindu

Table of Contents

2000-Present

The American Hindu

The American Hindu is a dynamic, youth-driven initiative that began as an informational Instagram page in January 2020. Seeing a lack of informative content on Hindu culture, Hindu-American students and young professionals from around the country came together to fill the void on social media. Focusing on education and advocacy of Hindu topics, the page features several post series such as Hinduism 101, Sanskrit Non-Translatables, Festival Posts, and Trending Topics.

The American Hindu has since evolved into a self-publishing organization specializing in a diverse range of Hindu educational content. Through a blend of traditional and modern mixed-media formats, including print and digital publications, videos, and interactive resources, the organization aims to make Hindu culture, philosophy, and history accessible and engaging for a wide audience. By empowering young creators and fostering a collaborative environment, The American Hindu preserves and promotes cultural heritage and encourages the exploration and understanding of Hindu traditions in a contemporary context.

The Hindu-American Mosaic

The Hindu-American Mosaic is the inaugural publication from The American Hindu, offering a tribute to the history and evolution of the Hindu community in the United States. Through recounts of various chapters of this multi-century history, this book delves into the diverse experiences and contributions of Hindu-Americans, celebrating their cultural heritage and impact on the broader American landscape.

The publication features writing by **Ashima Sharma**, illustrations by **Charu Chaturvedi**, special contributions by **Ishita Raghuvanshi** and **Ritika Devarakonda**, and the invaluable feedback and support of countless Hindu-Americans who inspire us everyday.

Foreword

Hinduism began to impact American culture long before Hindu people themselves settled in the country in significant numbers. A century and a half before the 1965 immigration reform opened the doors to Indians, Hindu texts and treatises about Hindu philosophy were changing the lives of prominent Americans like Ralph Waldo Emerson. The process accelerated with the procession of gurus, swamis, and yoga masters who came to the West, at first in a trickle, then a stream, then a flood.

Over time, ideas and practices born in ancient India contributed to the development of healthcare (e.g. doctors recommending yoga and meditation), psychology, neuroscience, theoretical physics, the arts, and most significantly, the way Americans understand and practice spirituality. I often say we're becoming a nation of yogis.

This was made possible because of the depth, breadth, and inclusivity of the Hindu tradition. No one was asked to convert to a new religion; Americans integrated core principles and methods(mainly of Vedanta and Yoga) into their lives on their own terms.

Foreword (contd.)

In recent decades another important factor was added: millions of citizens of Indian descent. Temples were erected, educational institutions were created, and many Indian-Americans achieved prominence in society. Indeed, as of this writing (August, 2024), we have a presidential candidate whose middle name is Devi.

I believe the transmission of Sanatana Dharma to the West has been one of most important developments in America's spiritual history. The concise overview in this book will help future generations fully appreciate that story.

-

Philip Goldberg

Philip Goldberg is the author of numerous books, including the award-winning *American Veda: From Emerson and the Beatles to Yoga and Meditation, How Indian Spirituality Changed the World*; the definitive biography, *The Life of Yogananda: The Story of the Yogi Who Became the First Modern Guru*; and his latest, *Spiritual Practice for Crazy Times*. He hosts the Spirit Matters podcast, leads American Veda Tours to India, conducts online courses and workshops, and contributes regularly to several publications. He is also an active board member of the Association for Spiritual Integrity.

Early
1800s

Influence of Hindu Thought in America

The impact of Hindu *Dharma* on transcendental philosophy can be traced back to the early 19th century when trade ships began sailing between ports in India and New England. This trade link between the two continents enabled cultural exchange which, along with the influence of Hindu teachings and sacred texts, left an impression on prominent transcendentalist writers and thinkers, including Ralph Waldo Emerson, Walt Whitman, and Henry David Thoreau.

The effect of Hindu ideas can be seen in the works produced by these writers. Emerson referred to Whitman's book, *Leaves of Grass*, as "a remarkable mixture of the *Bhagvat Ghita* [sic] and the *New York Herald*."[1] Similarly, Emerson drew inspiration from Hindu *Dharma* for the titles of many of his poems—including "Brahma" and "Maya." He included the concepts of the *Brahman*, the idea of rebirth, aspects of *Advaita* philosophy, as well as quotes from the *Bhagavad Gita* in many of his works.[2] Henry David Thoreau often spoke about the impact that reading Hindu scriptures, including the *Bhagavad Gita*, the *Vedas*, and the *Upanishads* had on his way of thinking and the work he produced. He felt that "Hindu scripture held 'the laws of you and me,' and gave him a novel way to conceptualize divinity's role in the material world." The influence of Hindu themes is present in all his works thereafter.[3]

Images (left to right): Henry David Thoreau; Ralph Waldo Emerson; Walt Whitman

1883

Breaking Glass Ceilings

Dr. Anandibai Joshi is considered to be the first Hindu woman to arrive in the United States, having arrived in 1883. She graduated from the Women's Medical College of Pennsylvania in 1886, becoming the first female of South Asian origin to hold a degree in Western medicine from the US.[4]

When Joshi's husband, Gopal, was exploring avenues for Joshi to come to America, one of his letters ended up being published in a January 1879 edition of the *Missionary Review*, alongside a letter from the editor discouraging the idea of an "unconverted Hindu in America." Later, this edition was read by a lady named Theodicia Carpenter from New Jersey, who was inspired to offer Joshi her own home for lodging. Before arriving in the United States, Joshi and Carpenter exchanged letters, in which Joshi related her way of life, shared Hindu customs, and emphasized the importance of her religion to her, stating, "I wish to preserve my manners and customs…Can I live in your country as if it were my own, and what will it cost me?"[5] Joshi had always made clear her intentions to remain true to her faith, declaring to the doubtful society in India, "I propose to myself to make no change in my customs and manners, food or dress. I will go as a Hindu, and come back here to live as a Hindu." She also addressed the question many had of her— why did she need to do what no other woman was doing? Dr. Joshi stated, "Society has a right to our work as individuals." Thus, Dr. Joshi set sail for her further education in America. She successfully completed her studies and returned to India to serve her community as a Hindu doctor.

Images (top to bottom): Anandibai Joshi with Kei Okami and Sabat Islambooly of the Woman's Medical College of Pennsylvania; site where Anandibai Joshi's ashes were laid to rest in New York

1893

Sisters and Brothers of America

Swami Vivekananda's visit to the 1893 World's Parliament of Religions in Chicago had a great influence on the perception of Hindu *Dharma* in America. His speech at the Parliament, famously beginning with the greeting, "Sisters and Brothers of America," along with other speeches over the next two years, covered universal spirituality, tolerance, and the oneness of all religions. They inspired many Americans and paved the way for the establishment of Vedanta Societies across the US, which continue to flourish now. Swami Vivekananda's teachings inspired many leaders, including the notable John. D. Rockefeller, among others.[6]

Rockefeller had previously been encouraged to meet Vivekananda by his peers, but only went to meet him when his health was severely declining. Meeting with Swami Vivekananda at this critical time sparked the beginning of Rockefeller's philanthropy.[7] Swami Vivekananda helped Rockefeller realize he would not be able to take any of his wealth with him to the grave. He wrote, "This is the chief sin—Selfishness, thinking of ourselves first. He who thinks 'I will eat first, I will have more money than others, and I will possess everything; he who thinks I will get to heaven before others, I will get to *Mukti* before others,' is the selfish man. The unselfish man says 'I will be last, I do not care to go to heaven, I will even go to hell, if by doing that I can help my brothers'."[8]

Images (top to bottom): Vivekananda at the first Parliament of World's Religions; A portrait of Swami Ji

1906

The First Hindu Temple in the Whole Western World

The first Vedanta Society, the Vedanta Society of New York, was founded by Swami Vivekananda in November 1894. He sent Swami Abhedananda to lead the organization in 1897. When Swami Vivekananda established the Vedanta Society of Northern California in San Francisco, he sent Swami Turiyananda to teach the group, who he said was "Vedanta personified," and would "help [all the disciples] to live pure and holy lives."[9] This center was advertised as the "first Hindu Temple in the Whole Western World" since 1906.[10]

Presently, there are fifteen Vedanta Society centers in the U.S. Each center is an official branch of the Ramakrishna Order, the monastic organization established by Swami Vivekananda in India.[11]

Images (left to right): Swami Vivekananda on the porch of Ridgely Manor during the "Great Summer" of 1899; The first Vedanta Center in the West, comprised of two rented rooms on 33rd St. in Manhattan

1907

Asiatic Exclusion League

The majority of Indian immigrants to the US in the late 1800s and early 1900s were Sikhs. At this time, anti-Asian sentiment was growing in America. Sections of the white American population did not like competing with immigrant laborers for work and tensions rose among the groups, culminating in an attack on the homes of 250 Sikh mill-workers in Bellingham, Washington by a mob of 600 white lumberjacks.[12] The actions of the mob were generally disapproved of, but many people supported the sentiment behind their attack. These immigrants were verbally abused regularly, commonly called "ragheads." Even in the articles covering the event, the Sikhs were referred to as "dusky aliens." In addition to riots, there were aggressions against immigrants in all avenues of life, with some brokers publicly pledging not to sell property to "Hindoos or Negroes."

The anti-Asian sentiment that had previously targeted Japanese and Korean immigrants was aimed at these South Asian immigrants as well—the anti-immigrant group called the Japanese and Korean Exclusion League changed its name to the Asiatic Exclusion League (AEL) to widen its exclusion agitation to include all "Asiatics—Indians." Soon after, California passed the Alien Act of 1913, in which any aliens who were not eligible for citizenship were barred from owning land. In 1917, the Barred Zone Act was passed by Congress, which halted immigration from many places, including India.

Images (left to right): Sikh laborers boarding a train in Canada; Damage following anti-Asian riots in Vancouver's Japan Town

1923

United States v. Bhagat Singh Thind

The United States v. Bhagat Singh Thind case was a landmark Supreme Court case in 1923. The case decided that Bhagat Singh Thind, a Sikh immigrant from India, was not eligible for US citizenship because he was not considered a "white person," according to the immigration laws of the time. [13]

This ruling contradicted the logic previously established by the Supreme Court in the Ozawa v. US case, which categorized Asian Indians as white. The Supreme Court said that the words "free white person" in the Naturalization Act were "words of common speech, to be interpreted in accordance with the understanding of the common man, synonymous with the word 'Caucasian' only as the word is popularly understood." [14]

At this time, immigration was largely limited to people from the British Isles and Northwestern Europe, so the previous ruling that provided American citizenship to any "any alien being a free white person", the court intended to describe European immigrants. This resolution led to about 50 other Indians, primarily Hindus and Sikhs, who had already been naturalized, being retroactively stripped of their citizenship after prosecutors argued that they had gained their citizenship illegally. This case brought up a contradictory duality—Asian Americans using proximity to whiteness to be accepted, and the US government using that same label to differentiate them. [15]

Images (left to right): A portrait of Bhagat Singh Thind; Bhagat Singh Thind and his wife Vivian Thind

1946

Yoga Comes to America

The origins of American yoga can be traced back to the mid-20th century, when Indian yogis and spiritual teachers, such as Paramahamsa Yogananda and Maharishi Mahesh Yogi, began to visit and teach in the United States.

Yogananda's arrival in the 1920s marked a significant milestone, as he founded the Self-Realization Fellowship (SRF). He also introduced many Americans to the practices of yoga and meditation through his teachings and writings, including his famous book "Autobiography of a Yogi" published in 1946.[16] His book had a profound impact on many including Steve Jobs. Jobs arranged for the book to be distributed to all that attended his memorial service after he passed away in October 2011. [17]

In 1927, he was also notably the first prominent Indian to be hosted in the White House, by President Calvin Coolidge. This helped to popularize yoga and spirituality in America and laid the groundwork for the growth of the modern yoga movement.

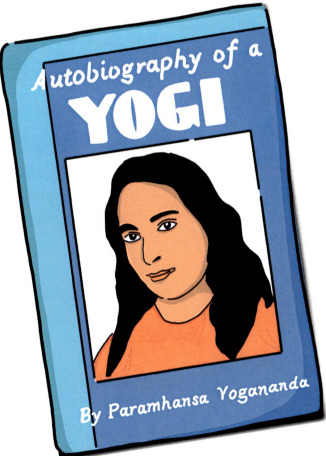

Image: Paramhansa Yogananda

1946

Immigration Reform

In 1946, along with the repeal of the Chinese Exclusion Act, the Luce-Celler Act extended naturalization rights and immigration quotas to India and the Philippines, both of which gained their independence from Great Britain and the United States respectively.[18] Following this, immigration increased from South Asia to the US. Over the next 20 years, almost 8,000 South Asians immigrated to the US. The Luce-Celler Act also permitted South Asians to become US citizens through naturalization.[19]

The India League of America, under the leadership of J. J. Singh, played a pivotal role in the passage of the Luce-Celler Act. The organization lobbied Congress, raised awareness about existing discriminatory immigration policies, and mobilized public opinion to support legislative change. Their advocacy marked a significant step toward greater immigration equality.[20]

Images (left to right): Harry Truman signing the Declaration of Emergency to initiate involvement in the Korean War; Harry Truman signing the Luce-Celler Act

1965

The Immigration and Nationality Act

The Immigration and Nationality Act of 1965 had a significant impact on Indian Americans as it eliminated quotas based on nationality and prioritized skilled immigrants, described as "those who can contribute most to this country—to its growth, to its strength, to its spirit."[21] This act opened more opportunities for Hindu professionals to immigrate to the United States, generating a large influx of Indian immigrants and contributing to the growth of the Hindu-American community.

Images (left to right): Lyndon B. Johnson signing the Immigration and Nationality Act of 1965; Immigrants in Ellis Island in 1965

1965

The Hare Krishna Movement

Srila Prabhupada arrived in New York in 1965 with an aim to share the teachings of *Bhakti Yoga* with the world. One year later, in July 1966, The International Society for Krishna Consciousness (ISKCON) was founded.[22]   This was the first encounter with a *swami* and the practice of chanting a *mahamantra* for many Americans. Soon, the *mantra* and the Hare Krishna Movement swept through the West. George Harrison, of The Beatles, was an early follower of ISKCON.[23] In 1970, Harrison produced the Radha Krishna Temple album with other devotees, and he soon bought a house and donated it as a center for the movement. This center was called the Bhaktivedanta Manor in honor of Swami Prabhupada.

ISKCON now includes 500 major centers, temples and rural communities, almost 100 affiliated vegetarian restaurants, thousands of *namahattas* or local meeting groups, a wide variety of community projects, and millions of congregational members worldwide. The New Vrindaban center in West Virginia spans over 2,500 acres and is recognized as an unincorporated town of its own. At this center, festivals, conferences, courses, and retreats are held, and thousands of devotees visit each year.[24]

Images (clockwise): Srila Prabhupada; Srila Prabhupada on the streets of New York in 1966; Srila Prabhupada sharing a laugh with ISKCON devotees

1967

Neem Karoli Baba

Neem Karoli Baba was a Hindu *guru*, widely known outside of India for guiding a number of Americans who had traveled to India in the 1960s and 1970s—some of the more prominent being Ram Dass, Bhagavan Das, and Krishna Das.[25] Other followers of Neem Karoli Baba include Steve Jobs, Mark Zuckerberg, and Larry Brilliant.[26]

Ram Dass was a Harvard psychologist and first went to India in 1967 and met his guru, Neem Karoli Baba. Once he returned to the US, he immersed himself in *bhakti yoga* focused on *Hanuman* and soon started the Hanuman Foundation, a non-profit which later branched off into the Human Kindness Foundation and the Living/Dying Project. Later, he founded the Seva Foundation, an international service organization.[27] Bhagavan Das met Neem Karoli Baba in 1965. Along with his wife, Amulya Maa, he runs programs to mentor *yoga* practitioners who want to deepen their *sadhana*. Bhagavan Das has also released many devotional tracks. Krishna Das first met Ram Dass, and through him, learned of Neem Karoli Baba. Krishna Das originally wanted to spend the rest of his life with Neem Karoli Baba in Kainchi, India, but Neem Karoli Baba sent him back to the US. In 1994, Krishna Das established a *kirtan* residency in New York City at the Jivamukti Yoga Center. Krishna Das has developed a signature style of singing and established the Kirtan Wallah Foundation in 2014 to spread the tradition of *kirtan*.
[28]

Images (left to right): Ram Dass; Ram Dass with his guru Neem Karoli Baba

Transcendental Meditation

Maharishi Mahesh Yogi was a Hindu *guru* that introduced Transcendental Meditation (TM) to the United States in the 1960s. TM involves the silent repetition of a mantra, promotes relaxation, reduces stress, and enhances overall well-being.

The practice quickly gained popularity, attracting numerous followers, including celebrities such as Jerry Seinfeld as well as the members of The Beatles and The Roling Stones. Its impact led to a broader interest in Eastern spirituality and alternative wellness practices, influenced the cultural and social landscape of the time, and led to the establishment of a network of TM centers across the country. Maharishi Mahesh Yogi's teachings helped to integrate meditation into mainstream American culture.[29]

In 1973, the Maharishi International University, founded by Maharishi Mahesh Yogi, opened in Goleta, California with the aim of incorporating the principles of Transcendental Meditation in higher education. A year later, the University was moved to a campus in Fairfield, Iowa.[30]

Images (left to right): Maharishi Mahesh Yogi in Fairfield, Iowa; Maharishi Mahesh Yogi with prominent artists including members of The Rolling Stones

1972

Ugandan Hindu Exodus

In 1972, over 70,000 Asians living in Uganda were ordered to leave within just 90 days, by dictator Idi Amin. He announced that in a dream he was told by Allah that Asians had to go, and he selectively expelled Hindus along with other Asians.[31] In 1894, when Uganda was still under British rule, many Indians had been brought to the country to help build railroads. The immigrants the British brought were mainly poor and uneducated from famine-prone areas. The expelled Hindus mass-migrated to the UK, India, Canada, and the US. Following this expulsion, Uganda faced a major shortage of skilled professionals, such as doctors, nurses, teachers, and bankers, which triggered a financial crisis and collapse of businesses.

Images (left to right): Ugandan refugees entering Canada; Ugandan refugees

1974

BAPS *Mandir* in NY Inaugurated

Bochasanwasi Shri Akshar Purushottam Swaminarayan Sanstha (BAPS) is a socio-spiritual Hindu faith and was developed by Bhagwan Swaminarayan in the early 1800s in Gujarat, India.[32] The faith spread steadily and *mandirs* were inaugurated in India, as well as in London and Nairobi. BAPS emphasizes the importance of *mandirs* as hubs for the community and centers of spiritual growth, as well as serving as a home away from home. This sentiment is even more powerful for Hindus that have migrated away from their ancestral homes.

The BAPS Swaminarayan Sanstha has built more than 1100 *mandirs* around the world. In August 1974, Pramukh Swami Maharaj, the fifth spiritual guru of the BAPS organization, inaugurated the first BAPS *mandir* in the US in New York. This establishment provided an avenue for connection and collaboration with the US as a whole. In 2000, during a visit to Miami to lay the foundation stone of a new *mandir*, Pramukh Swami Maharaj also met with President Clinton.

Images (clockwise): Pramukh Swami Maharaj and Bill Clinton; Pramukh Swami Maharaj inaugurating the first BAPS mandir in the US; Pramukh Swami Maharaj and community members at the inauguration

1970s

Popularizing Yoga

Although yoga was introduced in the US in the 1940s, the use of props such as blocks, straps, and blankets to help students access and deepen their poses greatly helped popularize yoga. B. K. S. Iyengar, who developed Iyengar Yoga, introduced such props. His emphasis on precise alignment and attention to detail helped to popularize yoga as a form of therapy and rehabilitation in the United States, which has persisted to this day.

In the 1970s, Bikram Choudhury developed Bikram Yoga, a hot yoga practice that consists of a specific sequence of 26 postures practiced in a room heated to 105 degrees Fahrenheit. Both Iyengar and Bikram's impact on yoga in America can be seen in the popularity of their respective styles and in the continued growth of the yoga industry in the United States.

Despite this, yoga has gained a strong following in the United States. A recent study estimated there are about 30 million yoga practitioners in America. In 2021, the market size of Pilates and yoga studios in the US amounted to nearly 9.9 billion US dollars. Overall, there were about 39 thousand yoga and Pilates businesses in the US in 2021.[33]

Images (left to right): B.K.S. Iyengar instructing Mary Dunn in Pune; B.K.S. Iyengar leading a yoga class

1977

Building *Mandirs*: Building Communities

The Flushing Hindu Temple, also known as the Hindu Temple Society of North America, was founded in 1970 by a group of Hindu immigrants in Flushing, Queens, New York. Initially, the *mandir* operated out of a small storefront, but as its membership grew, the community began fundraising efforts to build a larger *mandir*.

Notably, the late Mr. Alagappa Alagappan helped to garner support and organized the effort for this *mandir*. He chose the site of the *mandir* to be on Bowne Street. The street was named after John Bowne, a man who fought for the right for Quakers and followers of other religions to worship freely in the state of New York in the 17th century, when New York was still a Dutch colony.[34]

The *mandir* was not easily accepted in society, but the founder focused on the values of acceptance, even designing the original logo for the Hindu Temple Society of North America to contain symbols of all the major religions surrounding a *diya* (oil lamp) symbolizing knowledge.[35]

In 1977, a new *mandir* was constructed on the same site, featuring traditional Indian architectural elements and a central courtyard with a marble statue of *Bhagwan Ganesha*. This *mandir* is the second-oldest *mandir* built in the US. Today, there are around 1500 mandirs in the US, serving a Hindu population that has increased over thirtyfold since the Flushing Hindu Temple's construction.

Images (left to right): The Sri Maha Vallabha Ganapati Devasthanam in Queens, NY; Ganesh Chaturthi celebrations at the Flushing Hindu Temple

1970s

Hindu Community Organizes

With the growth of the Hindu community in the United States, several Hindu organizations grew branches in the US as well.

Vishwa Hindu Parishad of America (VHPA) was founded in New York in 1970. While sharing many of the same ideals, VHPA is legally and operationally independent of Vishwa Hindu Parishad of Bharat. VHPA aims to bring together the Hindu community and address issues they face in the US. Many initiatives focus on imparting Hindu culture and knowledge to children, including Hindu Heritage Camps, Hindu Students Council, and Balavihar with Chinmaya Mission. [36]

Chinmaya Mission was founded in 1953 by followers of Swami Chinmayananda in India. There are now devotees and centers all around the world, with programs for spiritual development. Balavihar focuses on children's education in Vedanta, promoting the development of strong Hindu values and cultural identity. [37]

Hindu Swayamsevak Sangh – USA (HSS USA) is another international organization that aims to coordinate the Hindu American community and practice, preserve, and advance the ideals and values of Hindu *Dharma*. With 220 branches nationwide (as of 2024) HSS conducts regular programs for children, youth, and families with games, exercise, and discussions on relevant topics, along with service activities and community outreach projects. [38]

Images (left to right): HSS Camp; Balavihar

The Dotbusters

The Dotbusters were a Hinduphobic hate group that emerged in Jersey City, New Jersey in 1987 and remained active until 1993. They specifically targeted Hindu Americans, particularly those who wore *bindis* on their foreheads. The group used violent and threatening tactics to intimidate and harm Hindu Americans, including physical assault and vandalism of property. One note left by the group threatened, "We will go to any extreme to get Indians to move out of Jersey City." [39] It was thought that this resentment towards the Indian immigrants was caused by the community's increasing affluence, as Jersey City was made up largely of other minority immigrant groups.

The Dotbusters' actions were widely condemned by the broader community, and the perpetrators were brought to trial for their crimes. The mandatory penalty in New Jersey for "bias crimes" was also raised after a group called Indian Youth Against Racism (IYAR) based at Columbia University documented instances of violence against Indians in New Jersey. These activities eventually led to increased awareness of, and efforts to combat, anti-Hindu sentiments in the United States. [40]

Image: Indian-American community members protest against racially motivated hate crimes

1990s

Tech Trailblazers

The migration of Hindus to the United States for work in the Information Technology (IT) industry has been a significant phenomenon in the late 1990s. Many Hindu professionals have migrated to the US to work in the tech sector and have contributed significantly to the country's economy and technological advancements. Many Hindu Americans have started their own companies, which have become major players in the tech industry. The Indian-American community is among the most educated and highest-earning ethnic groups in the US. [41]

Some notable figures who have broken through invisible barriers and established the Hindu-American community on the global stage include: Kalpana Chawla, an Indian-born American astronaut and aerospace engineer who was the first woman of Indian origin to fly to space; Sundar Pichai, CEO of Alphabet, Inc.; Indra Nooyi, CEO of PepsiCo; and Satya Nadella, CEO of Microsoft, among many others.

Images (left to right): Kalpana Chawla; Satya Nadella; Sunita Williams

2000

Congress Hindu Prayer

On September 14, 2000, Venkatachalapathi Samudrala, a Hindu priest from the Shiva Vishnu Hindu Temple in Parma, Ohio, delivered a prayer to the House in conjunction with Indian Prime Minister Atal Bihari Vajpayee's address to a joint meeting of Congress. He was the first Hindu ever to give the House invocation. Samuldrala ended his invocation with the *Shanti Mantra* from the *Upanishads*. He came as the guest of Rep. Sherrod Brown of Ohio, who thanked Samuldrala for the prayer, saying, "while we may differ in culture and traditions, we are all alike in the most basic aspiration of peace and righteousness." [42]

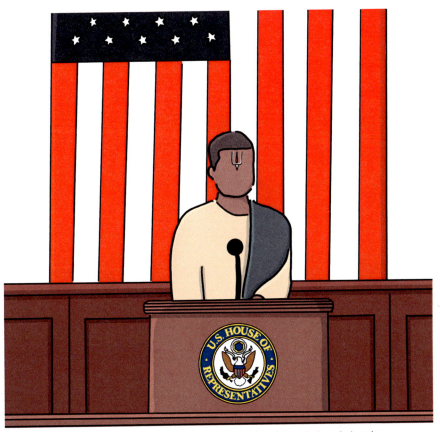

Images (left to right): Atal Bihari Vajpayee addressing Congress; Venkatachalapathi Samudrala with congressmen; Tulsi Gabbard lights the ceremonial diya at the Capitol Hill Diwali event in 2018

2003

First *Diwali* in the White House

Over 100 Hindu community members attended the first *Diwali* celebration at the White House in 2003, which was held in the Indian Treaty Room and presided over by Karl Rowe, President George W. Bush's chief political advisor. The festival was celebrated through the ceremonial lighting of a brass lamp.[43]

President Barack Obama continued the tradition and was the first president to personally celebrate *Diwali* in 2009, holding an event in the East Room. He also lit the first-ever *diya* in the Oval Office.

President Donald Trump also continued the tradition for some of his years in office. President Joe Biden held the largest *Diwali* celebration at the White House, followed by a *Diwali* reception at Vice President Kamala Harris's residence.[44]

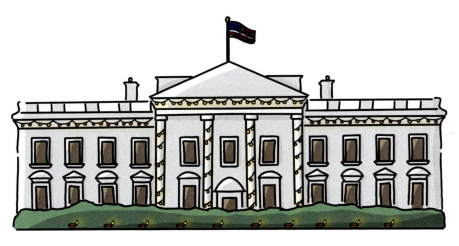

Images (left to right): Obama celebrates Diwali at the White House in 2016; Trump lights the ceremonial diya at the White House Diwali celebration in 2018; Biden hosts Diwali at the White House in 2022

Early
2000s

Arts

Hindu arts in America have found a significant audience across the United States since the late 20th century, facilitated by major festivals and artists.

The Cleveland Thyagaraja Festival, in Cleveland, Ohio, is the largest Indian classical music festival outside India with over 10,000 attendees.[45] Spanning 12 days annually around early April, the festival honors the revered composer Thyagaraja and features performances of *Carnatic* and *Hindustani* music as well as traditional dance forms such as *Bharatanatyam* and *Kuchipudi*.[46] Similarly, the Festival of Tabla in Aliso Viejo, California, is the largest gathering of Indian classical musicians on the West Coast and brings together a diverse array of *tabla* performances, educational workshops, and cultural discussions.[47] In New York City, the All Indian Dance Festival at Carnegie Hall celebrates the various Indian dance forms, showcasing classical and folk dance styles such as *Bharatanatyam*, *Kathak*, and *Garba*.[48]

Pandit Ravi Shankar introduced American audiences to Sitar and the textures of Hindustani classical music, influencing the fusion of Eastern and Western musical traditions. His collaboration with musicians like George Harrison of The Beatles helped popularize the sitar in American music.[49]

Additionally, hundreds of music and dance academies in the country illustrate the rich tapestry of Hindu arts in America.

Images (left to right): Ranjani and Gayatri at the Cleveland Thyagaraja Festival; Pandit Ravi Shankar with Georgia Harrison; Performers at the All India Dance Festival

2000s

Hindu Communities Grow

According to the Pew Research Center, the Hindu population in the US grew from approximately 1 million in 2000 to approximately 2.23 million in 2010, representing a growth rate of 115%. This growth was fueled by both immigration and high birth rates among Hindu families in the US.[50]

The growth of the Hindu population in America in the 2000s was also characterized by a more diverse spread of the community across the country. While Indian-Americans continued to be concentrated in traditional centers such as California, New York, and New Jersey, there was a significant increase in the number of Hindu communities in states such as Texas, Illinois, and Florida. This spread of the community was driven by factors such as job opportunities, affordable housing, and the desire for a better quality of life.

Images (left to right): Holi at the Radha Krishna Temple in Spanish Fork, Utah; Maha Kumbhabhishekam ceremony at the Hindu Temple Society of North America

2010s

Representation in Media and Politics

In the 1990s, Hindu representation in the media often played into Hindu and Indian stereotypes, as in the cases of Apu from "The Simpsons" and Ravi from Disney's "Jessie." Slowly, this evolved into mainstream portrayals of Hindu culture, however the actual beliefs behind many practices were sidelined. For example, the cartoon "Mira, Royal Detective" depicted *Diwali* and all the customs associated with it, such as making *rangoli*, eating sweets, and lighting *diyas*, however without any mention of *Bhagwan Ram*.[51] There is also notable Hindu representation in the show "Never Have I Ever", created by Mindy Kaling, which presents the characters' 'Hindu-ness' as an essential trait that makes them who they are. [52]

In politics, Tulsi Gabbard made history as she was sworn in as a member of the 113th Congress—the first Hindu ever elected to the House of Representatives. She opted to be sworn in on a *Bhagavad Gita*, saying "I chose to take the oath of office with my personal copy of the *Bhagavad Gita* because its teachings have inspired me to be a servant-leader, dedicating my life in the service of others and to my country."

Images (left to right): Mindy Kaling in The Office; Tulsi Gabbard taking her oath on her Bhagavad Gita; Apu from The Simpsons

Hinduphobia

Hinduphobia is defined as a set of antagonistic, destructive, and derogatory attitudes and behaviors towards *Sanatana Dharma* (Hindu *Dharma*) and Hindus that may manifest as prejudice, fear, or hatred.[53] Hinduphobia in the United States has been widely evident in universities. One incident involved Audrey Truschke, an Associate Professor of South Asian History at Rutgers University. Truschke repeatedly used vulgar language to describe *Bhagwan Ram* and *Sita* to recount events in the *Ramayana*, among other affronts. In 2021, Hindu groups, including Hindu YUVA, Hindu Students Council, and the Hindu American Foundation demanded an apology from Truschke.[54]

Hinduphobia has tied in with pushback against *"Hindutva"*, a term that is meant to be "more expansive than the religious aspects of Hindu *Dharma*, encompassing the cultural, linguistic, political, and social aspect of the Hindu people," as coined by V.D. Savarkar.[55] However, this term is now used in a negative light for any Hindus advocating against Hinduphobia, or Hindus running for office, being labeled "Hindu supremacists." In September 2021, the University of Chicago held a conference, "Dismantling Hindutva," and was advertised as a collaboration with many universities. However, when the Coalition of Hindus of North America (CoHNA) followed up with university leadership, it was found that seals of many universities were used without their knowledge. "We were previously unaware that UMass Boston was listed as a co-sponsor and we have not formally received any request," said the UMass Boston Chancellor.[56]

DOTHEAD
SUPERSTITIOUS
NATIONALIST
PAJEET
BACKWARD
HEATHEN
IDOL
COW PISS
WORSHIPPER
DRINKER
INFIDEL
FASCIST

Images (left to right): The Hindu Temple and Cultural Centre in Bothell, Washington following vandalism in 2015; Graphic used in the "Dismantling Hindutva" conference

2018

World Hindu Congress

In 2018, the World Hindu Congress (WHC), a global platform for Hindus to connect and collaborate, was held in Chicago as a tribute to the 125th anniversary of Swami Vivekananda's speech in Chicago at the Parliament of Religions in 1893. The inaugural WHC in 2014 was held in Delhi, India, followed by WHC 2018 in Chicago, and WHC 2023 in Bangkok, Thailand. The theme of the 2018 conference was *"Sumantrite Suvikrante*: Think Collectively, Achieve Valiantly." WHC 2018 was attended by 2,500 Hindus from 60 countries, and there were sizable delegations from India and the United States. [57] Attendees included: Sri Sri Ravi Shankar, the founder of the Art of Living Foundation; His Holiness the 14th Dalai Lama, Honorable Shri Mohan Bhagwat, from Rashtriya Swayamsevak Sangh; and Congressman Raja Krishnamoorthi. [58]

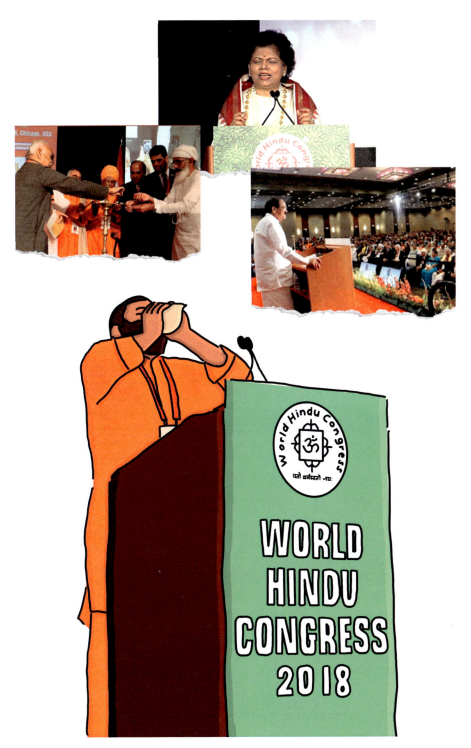

Images (left to right): Mohan Bhagwat inaugurates the World Hindu Congress; Chandrika Tandon performs the Ekatmata Mantra; Former Vice President of India Venkaiah Naidu speaks at WHC

2021

Hindu Heritage Month

Virginia became the first state to formally recognize October as Hindu Heritage Month in 2022, and every succeeding year. Since 2013, the Hindu American Foundation has led efforts to recognize October as Hindu American Awareness and Appreciation Month (HAAAM) as part of the global Hindu Heritage Month campaign. October is the month in which many major Hindu festivals are celebrated, including *Navratri* and *Diwali*. In the years since, several states, including Georgia, Michigan, Florida, New Jersey, Nevada, Ohio, Pennsylvania, and many more, have recognized Hindu Heritage Month with proclamations. [59]

The recognition of Hindu Heritage Month is important because it increases awareness about the practices of Hindu *Dharma*, similar to Asian American and Pacific Islander Month, among others. Proclamations at the local level are stepping stones to nationwide recognition and awareness.

STATE OF ARIZONA
★
COMMENDATION

WHEREAS, Arizona is proud of its rich cultural history and the many people who call our state home; and

WHEREAS, Hinduism is one of the largest practiced religions in the world; and

WHEREAS, the Hindu heritage, culture, traditions, and values have enriched our great state by providing invaluable solutions and often serve as a source of inspiration; and

WHEREAS, Hindu-Americans, many who live in Arizona, have made significant contributions across all fields, including science, education, medicine, law, politics, business, culture, sports, and more; and

WHEREAS, during the month of October 2022, the Hindu community across the State of Arizona and across our great nation will collectively celebrate its heritage by focusing on its culture and the diverse spiritual traditions rooted in India.

NOW, THEREFORE, I, Douglas A. Ducey, Governor of the State of Arizona, do hereby extend greetings and best wishes to all observing October 2022 as

HINDU HERITAGE MONTH

IN WITNESS WHEREOF, I have hereunto set my hand and caused to be affixed the Great Seal of the State of Arizona

GOVERNOR

DONE at the Capitol in Phoenix on this sixteenth day of August in the year Two Thousand and Twenty-Two, and of the Independence of the United States of America the Two Hundred and Forty-Seventh

ATTEST:

SECRETARY OF STATE

Images (left to right): Arizona Proclamation for Hindu Heritage Month; Georgia Governor Brian Kemp declares October as Hindu Heritage Month

2023

Akshardham

Construction began in Robbinsville, NJ, for a BAPS Shri Swaminarayan *Mandir* in 2010. This *mandir* was the second phase of the Hindu American Religious Center construction. The *mandir* itself was completed in 2014, and was inaugurated at this time, but construction continued on the surrounding campus and the Akshardham structure itself, which was completed in October 2023. In Sanskrit, "*Akshardham*" means "an eternal place." BAPS also has *Akshardham* complexes in Gandhinagar, Gujarat, and Delhi, India. The Robbinsville *Akshardham* is the second-largest Hindu *mandir* outside of India, following only Angkor Wat in Cambodia. It is the largest place of Hindu worship in the United States, spanning over 185 acres.

The construction of this *mandir* was completed through the efforts of 12,500 volunteers, guided by artisans from India, and is a testament to the dedication and belief of the BAPS community. The *mandir* also serves to commemorate the Hindu community in America and has several features paying tribute to the location. The *Brahma Kund* (stepwell) on the campus contains water from over 300 holy rivers and bodies of water in India, as well as water from each of the 50 states in the US.[60]

Images (left to right): Statue of Nilkanthvarni; Devotees place bricks at the Shilanyas Pujan; A volunteer cleans the temple structure

Endnotes

1. Rajasekharaiah, T.R. *The Roots of Whitman's Grass*. Rutherford: Fairleigh Dickinson UP, 1970.
2. Neupane, K. (2021). Ralph Waldo Emerson's Literary Works: A reflection of Hindu philosophy. *Cognition*, 3(1), 42-46. https://doi.org/10.3126/cognition.v3i1.55635
3. Raeder, Samantha. "Thoreau's Biophilia: The Influence of Hindu Scriptures on Walden's Portrayal of Nature and the Divine ." *University of Michigan*, 2017.
4. Dall, C. (1888). *The Life of Dr. Anandabai Joshee*. Roberts brothers.
5. Dall (n 4)
6. How Vivekanand Inspired John D Rockefeller - PANORAMA BusinessToday, n.d
7. Be a Trustee, NOT an Owner of Wealth | Vivekananda's Teaching to Rockefeller - The Spiritual Bee, n.d.
8. Vivekananda, 1892
9. Chetanananda, S. (1997). *God Lived with Them*.
10. *Impact on History—The Vedanta Society of New York*. (n.d.).
11. *History of the Vedanta Society of New York*. (n.d.). Vedanta Society of New York.
12. *Discrimination: The "Ragheads."* (n.d.).
13. Pillai, D. (n.d.). *United States v. Bhagat Singh Thind: Dual Legacies of a Forgotten Supreme Court Case*.
14. Coulson, D. (2017). *Race, Nation, and Refuge*.
15. Pillai (n 13)
16. *In America and across the world, India reclaims its yoga heritage—Times of India*. (n.d.).
17. Segall, L. (2013, September 10). Steve Jobs' last gift. CNN Money.
18. *Luce-Celler Act of 1946—Immigration History*. (n.d.).
19. *1946-1964: Restoration of Immigration and Citizenship | Pioneering Punjabis Digital Archive*. (n.d.).
20. Shaffer, R. (2012). J. J. Singh and the India League of America, 1945-1959: Pressing at the Margins of the Cold War Consensus. Journal of American Ethnic History.
21. *Immigration and Nationality Act*. (n.d.).
22. *Acharya: The Teacher of Teachers*. (n.d.).
23. *George Harrison - Bhaktivedanta Manor - Hare Krishna Temple Watford*. (n.d.).
24. *HISTORY*. (n.d.). New Vrindaban.
25. General 3. (n.d.). Neem Karoli Baba Ashram.
26. Gokhale, N. (2023, January 19). Neem Karoli Baba: Mystic who left footprints on the hearts and minds of Steve Jobs, Mark Zuckerberg. Scroll.in.
27. *About Ram Dass • Ram Dass*. (n.d.).
28. Bio. (n.d.). *Krishna Das*.
29. Weber, J. (2014). Transcendental meditation in america: How A new age movement remade a small town in Iowa. University of Iowa Press.
30. Narayanan, V. (n.d.). How Americans came to embrace meditation, and with it, Hindu Dharma.
31. Patel, H. H. (1972). General Amin and the Indian Exodus from Uganda.

32. What We Do. (n.d.). BAPS.
33. U.S. Americans who practiced yoga 2023. (n.d.). Statista.
34. Alagappa Alagappan, 88, Dies; Founded Hindu Temples Across U.S. - The New York Times. (n.d.).
35. Ecumenical Symbol for the Hindu Temple Society of North America. (n.d.).
36. VHPA History and Milestones - Vishwa Hindu Parishad of America. (n.d.).
37. About Chinmaya Mission. (n.d.).
38. About Us. (2024, April 15). HSSUS.
39. In Jersey City, Indians Protest Violence–The New York Times. (n.d.).
40. Dot Busters in New Jersey. (2009, February 11).
41. Kochhar, R., & Cilluffo, A. (2018, July 12). Income inequality in the U.S. is rising most rapidly among Asians. Pew Research Center.
42. Proceedings and Debates of the 106th Congress, Second Session: Hearing on 108, Congress 2 (2000).
43. The second edition of the Global Population Health Summit takes place in New York; Gender-related processes addressed–Times of India. (n.d.).
44. How The White House Has Celebrated Diwali Over The Years. (n.d.).
45. Cleveland Thyagaraja Festival. Cleveland Thyagaraja Festival. (n.d.).
46. 2024 Cleveland thyagaraja festival. , Aradhana Committee at Waetjen Auditorium @ Cleveland State University, Cleveland OH, Festivals. (n.d.).
47. Festival of Tabla. FOT 2024. (n.d.). https://www.festivaloftabla.com/
48. All Indian Dance Festival. All Indian Dance Festival. (n.d.).
49. Rothman, L. (2016, April 7). Pandit Ravi Shankar: How the sitar player won U.S. audiences. Time.
50. Pew Research Center. (2015, May 12). America's changing religious landscape. Pew Research Center.
51. Today, H. (2021, October 1). Hindu Dharma in the American Media. Hindu Dharma Today.
52. Bahl, D. (n.d.). Indian misrepresentation in media. El Estoque.
53. Working Definition. (n.d.).
54. Kumar, A. (n.d.). The Truschke Purana: A saga in Hinduphobia. The Times of India.
55. Shukla, S. (2021, October 5). What does Hindutva really mean? Hindu American Foundation.
56. Dismantling Global Hindutva (September 10–September 12, 2021) Virtual Event | South Asian Languages and Civilizations. (n.d.).
57. WHC 2018- World Hindu Congress. (n.d.).
58. World Hindu Congress 2018: State Heads, Chief Ministers, Global Business Leaders To Attend Mega Event In Chicago. (n.d.).
59. All About Hindu Heritage Month. (n.d.). Hindu American Foundation.
60. Discover | BAPS Swaminarayan Akshardham. (n.d.).

Our Inspiration

Goldberg, P. (2013). American Veda. Three Rivers Press.